AFTER THE SPLIT

The Definitive Guide to Recovery When Relationships Break Down

DANIELLE BARBEREAU

ISBN: 978-0-9931814-3-6

Danielle Barbereau danielle@danielleb.co.uk

Printed by Northend Creative Print Solutions, Sheffield

Acknowledgements

A huge thank you to those who made the writing of this book possible:

Clients: thank you for telling me your stories and trusting me to help you navigate the rough waters. What you have told me informed my work and can help other people too. I know that now you have all moved forward in your life. You are now safe and strong. You have moved to better things.

My thanks, gratitude and admiration.

Solicitors: Thank you Michaela Heathcote, Head of Family Law at Taylor and Emmet (LLP) in Sheffield, for providing the legal content I needed for this book. Thank you also to all solicitors who refer their clients to me. Without them, I simply could not have written the book. In particular, thank you to Michaela, again, and Alison Kitchman (Head of Family Law at Taylor Bracewell).

My friends: Thank you for being there for me at all times. Saying thank you does not begin to express my heartfelt gratitude.

To Ian Duffy and Dorothy Betts; thank you for reading over my initial efforts and making such useful comments and amendments. Thank you also for always being there for me and being my precious support network.

To Grace Oldfield; thank you for an inspired suggestion for the title.

To Janet Alton, friend and now business partner. For her continual support and for proofreading, editing and typesetting this book, with endless patience and ruthless attention to detail. I am glad that she thinks we make a good team. A great privilege for me.

Kim Morgan, who founded **Barefoot Coaching**: training with her changed the direction of my career and made me realise that coaching was my passion. As a coach and a woman, Kim inspired me and, no doubt, countless others.

My daughters: Anne-Claire and Fiona, who give meaning to my life and who have grown into happy, kind and well-adjusted young women. As a mother, I am brimming with pride and joy.

Contents

Introduction

Statistics show that the rate of divorce and separation that affects people in their 50s and 60s has increased by over 70% in the past 20 years, whereas it has decreased in other age groups. Reasons for this include:

- The loss of stigma over being divorced (including in later years)
- Women being more financially independent than in previous generations
- People often have much higher expectations about their lives than in previous generations
- Longer age expectancy: people in this age group know that they could be retired for a long time and feel entitled to some happiness
- The prospect of staying in a loveless relationship for another 25 years or more propels them to leave unsatisfactory relationships and open themselves to other possibilities in the future.

Still, no matter how common it may be, statistics do not reflect the feelings such personal tragedy brings into a person's life when, suddenly and unexpectedly, their partner drops the bombshell that they are leaving and that they do not love them any more and everything collapses around them.

Being abandoned by a partner really hurts you to the core. It does not matter how it happens, whether you are given an explanation for it, or if you are being dumped unceremoniously by text, or even without an explanation; when your partner turns away from the relationship you are left bereft, tortured and utterly lost.

Romantic rejection is unbelievably painful and leaves you feeling so devastated that you can only compare it with a form of mourning. Even if the relationship was not very good, you crave the presence of your partner. This is normal, and the loss can have a significant impact on your health and wellbeing. Going through a breakup can lead to sleeplessness, weight loss, high blood pressure and even chronic depression. When it happens, you naturally focus on how awful you feel and get stuck in your recollection of the breakup. The pain you feel is overwhelming and real. When attempting to describe how they feel, clients use words such as: 'I felt that my future had been ripped apart'; 'I went cold'; 'I could not breathe'; 'I felt I had been punched hard in the stomach'; 'I was shell-shocked'.

Yet rest assured that this feeling of pain and helplessness will eventually diminish and pass.

In fact, for many people, an unexpected breakup can mean the start of a new life. A paper in the *Journal of Positive Psychology* (2007) reported that when partners were not married, 'by 11 weeks after the split, nearly three quarters of respondents felt a sense of personal growth'. Even those going through a divorce felt that the period of acute pain was diminishing 'in a matter of months, not years'.

However, when you are in the midst of the crisis, it is hard to believe that you will ever get better. Also, even when the pain starts to abate, it does take time to make sense of what has happened and truly move on.

This book addresses both women and men in their 40s, 50s and above, who had expected to remain married into their old age. If you are in that age group and you are the one who has been left behind, you may be drowning in confusion. This book is intended to provide practical help and support for women and men who find themselves in this situation. It also relates their experiences at these difficult times. Rejected partners feel that they are completely alone, that they are drowning and have lost control, while their partner seems to be calling all the shots.

The overarching aim of this book is to help you to resurface and move on:

- How do you resurface when you are at rock bottom?
- Eventually how do you grow from the experience?

This book is designed to help both women and men because they all experience the same issues when their long-term partner leaves. Yet there are also differences. Women can experience a different set of problems. For example, men can leave their wives for younger women and have a new family, which is not always possible the other way round. Also in mid years, women experience the menopause, which is often a fraught time in terms of health and identity. However, women may have the ability to deal with problems differently because they are generally able to discuss emotional issues with close friends more easily than men. Therefore this book will focus on both women and men, as both groups can benefit from practical help and support at this time.

This book is primarily (but not exclusively) for you, if: -

- You are in your 40s and above
- You may have been in your relationship for a long time
- You may not be used to handling personal failure
- You still have to function at work
- You are possibly a parent of grown up children
- You have lost all that was familiar
- Your planned future has vanished
- Your children have flown the nest and started a new life
- Your partner has left you, possibly for a younger model
- You are going through your mid-life; a transitional and pivotal time raising many physical and mental issues at the best of times.

Throughout this book I have used examples of real clients, but have changed their names to preserve confidentiality. The experience of heartache and the devastating consequences a relationship breakdown can have on people's lives is both unique and universal. The purpose of this book is to make people realise that they are not alone during this time and that practical help and support is available.

Who am I to write this book?

I work with people going through relationship breakups

Over the last few years, I have worked with many clients who needed to gain clarity regarding their fractured relationship. This might mean seeing how they can change it for the better, or making the decision to end it.

I do not judge or try to tell people what they should do – apart from the odd nudge when they are stuck in unhelpful patterns – but I help clients make the choices which are right for them.

I adopt a positive dynamic approach, so when they work with me, clients feel better very quickly. Their feedback is unanimously heart-warming and it is a huge privilege to know that I have made a difference in their lives, at a time when they were so distraught and in need of support.

My support helps clients to:

- Survive times of personal crisis, such as divorce
- Discover strategies and tools to survive difficult breakups
- Rediscover who they are and what they want to do next
- Remain calm and reasonable in stressful situations
- Feel empowered, clear-headed and able to express what they want effectively
- Make relationships healthier, whether they decide to stay together or separate
- Reach the best possible outcome for them and their family while keeping control of legal timing and costs.

I want to share my experience, knowledge and expertise to help you too.

Some of my clients are initially referred to me by family solicitors who are committed to finding the best resolution for their clients, but most of my clients come to me by word of mouth.

I absolutely love doing what I do. Having worked in the University sector as a senior manager, feeling submerged in endless administrative tasks, I appreciate the privileged position my job brings, which is entirely about creating a unique, close and supportive relationship with clients. I do challenge them too, but this is to help them when they are stuck so they can make real progress.

I have been through the experience myself and remember how it feels.

1
'I don't love you any more; I am leaving'

How does it feel to be left?

- Total sense of rejection and uselessness
- Old and obsolete
- Loss of control over your own life
- Feeling that other people are calling the shots
- Powerless
- Fearful
- Deeply shocked
- Guilty
- Ashamed
- It's my fault
- Lonely
- Humiliated
- Confused
- Bewildered
- No sense of purpose
- Rudderless: no direction
- Loss of wellness: sleeplessness, confusion, weight loss or gain
- Financially worse off.

Where do you go from here?

In the midst of this chaos, you have to find a way of rediscovering who you are, what you want, and to create a new life, while you are dealing with potentially damaging emotions. Failure to do so will delay recovery and keep you feeling useless and obsolete.

You sit at home feeling rejected and that your life has been ripped apart at the worst possible time. The future can look very bleak and leave you not knowing how to move forward.

And yet, you can survive this. Not only that, you can get a better life.

This book will help you to:

- Survive the immediate aftermath of the breakup
- Make sense of what happened
- Regain control
- Deal with damaging emotions
- Learn from the experience
- Prepare to move forward in a positive way.

2
'This is going nowhere'

These ominous words, often spoken out of the blue, come as a complete shock. You may have been reasonably happy and convinced that you had a good marriage. Over time it may have felt dulled by the number of years spent together; less passionate, but still on the whole solid and comfortable. Thinking about it, you admit that along the years, there may have been a few signs that all was not perfect, but you had no idea that the cracks were so damaging. Your expectations were that the marriage was meant to endure. After all, you had weathered other difficult times in the past.

Over the years, you learnt to keep going by focusing on what is good in the relationship and ignoring the bad; that often helped. At difficult times, you may have wanted to preserve the marriage, as that was always the easier option. This may have involved compromise – walking on eggshells to avoid rocking the boat, at the expense of how you really felt. When working at the relationship, people don't normally consider that all the invested effort and emotions could lead to a breakup – sometimes at the very time when you and your partner should be looking forward to enjoying more quality time together after many years of putting others first.

The following pages will give examples of real situations experienced by some of my clients. You may find similarities within the examples that chime with your own experiences and circumstances.

You can't make someone love you.

Your partner had been preparing an exit for a long time

The words 'I don't love you any more; I am leaving' may come out of nowhere to you, but sometimes an exit is prepared years in advance:

> Viv, a lovely lady in her 50s, was told that now the children had left home, it was time to downsize. Her husband asked her to look for a new home for the couple to move to when the children left the nest, which she did, despite loving the family home and its cherished memories. Her husband said that it would be selfish of them to keep a large family home when they could help their children onto the property ladder if they downsized. The couple bought the smaller house, but the husband never moved in, and the children never got the money for a deposit on a property. The whole plan was part of a big strategy to leave her. He thought that it would be good enough to provide the new house for her as accommodation when he left. The realisation that he had planned his exit for years, when she had not suspected anything, was particularly difficult and humiliating for Viv. She also discovered that he was leaving her for a younger woman. She questioned the meaning of all their years together and felt that in fact she did not know her husband at all.

> Many partners do not even give the courtesy of an explanation; they just leave the marriage and their previous life behind and move on. Or it may seem that way on the surface.

You have been left without an explanation

You may have been jilted for example by:

- Text or note
- Perhaps you found an empty wardrobe when you got home after work
- You saw a removal van on the driveway
- Or maybe you heard absolutely nothing at all!

Unbelievable! Yet I have met clients to whom all of these things really happened. Not being given an explanation is certainly not unusual but it is infinitely cruel. Not only does it show a complete disregard for your feelings but also annihilates the value of the years you spent together. You are left wondering why. You blame yourself. This adds to the feeling of powerlessness, because you have no closure, let alone the opportunity to do anything to repair the relationship. After many years together, you feel you certainly deserve the respect of being given an explanation, but in many cases this will never happen.

There are many reasons for this, but generally speaking partners who behave like this are intrinsically cowardly and selfish. Even though, unbeknown to you, they had already decided to leave and had planned their departure, they don't want to be seen as the guilty party or to have to take responsibility for their own actions.

In cases like this you may ask: 'Why could he/she not tell me? Am I not even worthy of an explanation?' 'I would have understood'. The latter unfortunately is probably not true, but at least you would have had an opportunity to hear and to respond. However, your partner did not want to have to hear your response, or to engage with it, as this could have led to them having to take responsibility for their actions.

Many people avoid confrontation, sometimes thinking that it is better for their partner. How wrong they are: people are desperate for an explanation. The jilter may not be able to cope with the reality of seeing the consequences of their action. To be fair, very few people really want to see their partner suffer and be humiliated. Arguably their apparently heartless attitude is actually due to an overwhelming sense of guilt that they do not know how to express.

What is certain is that when someone decides that a relationship is over, it really is over. They may have been thinking about it for years, like Viv's husband. In their mind, it is old news, in which case a confrontation feels pointless. They would much rather see the matter as resolved and no longer discussed.

You have been told out of the blue that the relationship is over

Every client I work with is able to tell me exactly the moment and the manner in which they were told that the relationship was over, even years after the event. The words used to inform them of the end of their relationship are etched in their mind:

- 'I no longer love you; I am leaving'
- 'This is going nowhere'
- 'There is an elephant in the room'
- 'I can't do this any more'
- 'I cannot imagine growing old with you'

- 'It's over'
- 'I've met someone else'
- 'I am going to work and I am not coming back'.

Hearing something like this unexpectedly is shocking and can have a devastating effect. Often you do not even comprehend what your partner is talking about. In contrast, although you will be fighting hard to understand what you've just heard, the jilter seems to expect you to be very clear about what is happening. At this stage you have no idea that he/she has been contemplating this for some time.

To add to the sense of bewilderment, your partner may have seemed particularly attentive and loving before they dropped this bombshell. They certainly never gave any indication that they were unhappy with you or your relationship, so until that point you still believed all was well and that your marriage was secure.

Consequently this leaves you feeling that you have no opportunity to discuss the problems and try to find a solution. At this point the crushing news that your relationship is about to end leaves a yawning sense of hopelessness.

You are being cornered by your partner so you have no choice but to initiate the breakup

As well as the jilter who just disappears without a word of explanation due to their unwillingness to take any responsibility, there are others who push their partner into a corner so they have no choice but to initiate the breakup themselves. They throw their weight around, have affairs and create chaos, while still maintaining everything is normal. Again, they want to avoid being seen as the guilty party in the eyes of friends and relatives.

> Mark is a senior executive in his early 40s. He came to see me because he was suspecting that his wife of 20 years was having an affair. At no time did she admit to it. In fact when he questioned her about it she was adamant that he was imagining things, despite many signs to the contrary. This made Mark feel humiliated and foolish, because he had to deal with lies and deceit in addition to the rejection. In fact his wife's actions were blatant and typical of cheaters: mysterious phone calls, new care for her appearance, 'late nights' at the office, 'business conferences', moving to the spare room 'not to wake him', watching TV in a different room,

not spending time with their young children and then arranging exciting outings where her husband was not included.

Despite his efforts to discuss the situation and try to find a resolution, she insisted everything was normal and was unwilling to admit anything was wrong. Eventually he had to make the painful decision to end the marriage. She then told both sets of parents that Mark was divorcing her and that she didn't know why.

This form of breakup is very common, yet it is very cowardly and unfair. It leaves the injured party with no explanation, and no choice but to end the relationship for their own sanity. They end up feeling confused, worthless and having to deal with an enormous sense of guilt, especially if children are involved. While part of them would do anything to keep things as they were in the past and to convince their partner to stay, they realise deep down that this would not work, as the relationship has been damaged beyond repair and all trust has gone. Therefore they feel they have no option but to initiate proceedings and allow themselves to be portrayed as the guilty party by their partner.

Due to the nature of my work, I generally only deal with the injured party. I rarely deal with the partner creating the chaos, even though I would very much like to find out what they feel at that point. In my view, on some level they want to be found out, or even think that they can have the best of both worlds. It seems that they keep their options open for as long as possible and may even see their current partner as a safety net to fall back on if the exciting new relationship does not work out. Their callousness and disregard for their partner's feelings is extraordinary. Not surprisingly it takes a long time to recover from such a break.

3
The dressing gown:

THE IMMEDIATE AFTERMATH OF THE BREAKUP AND HOW IT AFFECTS OUR HEALTH AND SANITY

Many people recall the first few days after the shock announcement as a complete haze where they behave out of character. One recurring reaction is staying in bed, unable to move, not sleeping, not eating and sometimes even not washing. You stay in your dressing gown for days, not having the energy to get dressed. You experience a complete shutdown. As it goes on, you wonder if you will ever feel normal again. I remember a client in her 30s arriving in my office clutching a hot water bottle to her chest. She said that she could not warm up. Shock can have that effect; it can leave you cold, literally.

This is difficult too because most of the time you still have to function, to go to work, to deal with your children, family and friends who are also upset.

> Megan is a senior partner in a law firm. Her husband left her out of the blue, without telling her anything of his decision. She came home from work early one day to find a removal van on the drive and her husband taking his possessions away. He had not given her any indication of what he was about to do and certainly did not want to discuss anything as he was driving away. He did not open the van window, even when she was screaming and banging the door with her fists. Not surprisingly, she was utterly devastated. I'll always remember her opening the door to me in her dressing gown, saying that she did not have the strength to get out of bed and get dressed.
>
> *'My husband had just left me after over 20 years together. I was at rock bottom. I felt my future had been ripped from me and that life no longer had any meaning. I was unable to get out of bed in*

the morning and had even contemplated suicide. I hated myself for not being able to function and for others having to do more as a result. I simply could not carry on like this, but knowing that just added to the pressure'.

Going through an unexpected breakup at this time in your life can feel like falling into an endless black hole. Dealing with the aftermath of a sudden breakup is comparable to grieving. This is completely normal. Even if it seems implausible, bad times will pass.

Time to begin the grieving process.

So, what is grief?

Recovering from grief is a process which has to be gone through stage by stage. It is slow, it is painful, it is messy and sadly there are no shortcuts.

The stages of grief

The psychologist Elisabeth Kübler-Ross worked primarily with death and bereavement but her work helps us understand our emotional response to traumatic events. She identified five stages of grief:

1. Denial: you simply cannot accept that the breakup has occurred and you fantasise that the jilter will see the error of his/her way and come back to you

2. Anger: this takes many forms: thinking 'why me?', talking about the jilter's faults to others, destroying their possessions, being consumed by anger

3. Bargaining: despite all evidence you think that if you work at it, if you attempt to negotiate, threaten, assure your partner that you will change, then everything will be all right again. You ignore your sense of self-respect

4. Depression: because none of this works, you may feel exhausted, and left with a real feeling of hopelessness, believing that this state of misery will last for ever

5. Acceptance: finally you learn to make peace with your loss. You understand that your old life has gone and that you must now create a new reality for yourself.

None of this happens in a tidy straight line. We go through ups and downs, peaks and troughs. Besides, pain and grief, just like love, are personal emotions and no-one reacts exactly in the same way.

All we can do is realise that we are grieving, that the process is running its course.

Remember: **You will get better**.

It is worth remembering also that being with a partner for a long time affects our personality, whether we like it or not. New research confirms that we are affected by those we love. Falling in love changes us for better or for worse. When we fall in love we integrate aspects of our partner's personality. So when our partner leaves us, not only do we lose him/her but to some extent we lose part of our sense of self too.

No wonder that we feel completely confused and lost.

It is therefore essential to build a new sense of self: who am I and who do I want to be?

Dealing with such fundamental questions shows that recovery is a difficult process.

You will get better and you will find a new you.

4
From breakup to recovery

New beginnings are often disguised as painful endings.
Lao Tzu (Chinese philosopher, 571-531 BC, father of Toaism)

Top tips and thoughts, which are the results of many hours I spend working with people who are left bereft. Some may hopefully resonate with you:

- As bad as things seem at the moment, these times will pass
- Accept that the relationship is over: you deserve better
- Your partner will justify their actions no matter what and may never face up to what they have done. (They are not covering themselves in glory right now)
- Your partner is NOT coming back
- You may never know why they left
- You may never get the explanation or the apology you so richly deserve
- Just because they claim something, it doesn't make it true
- Accept where you are. Don't dwell on what you can't change. This will make moving forward easier
- Although your partner is no longer the person you used to love, it was not all bad; you were happy in the past
- You are going through life changing emotions; it's OK to feel these emotions
- Recovery takes time. You cannot just bounce back; you need to go through a process
- Be kind to yourself – no beating yourself up and taking all the responsibility
- Start thinking of you and your future
- Take control.

You can emerge a better, stronger and happier person, I PROMISE!

Emerging: starting to make sense of what is happening

Unfortunately most of us don't tend to seek advice on the best way to go about a breakup with a partner. Consequently people get hurt, when a lot of pain and suffering could be avoided.

In *Runaway Husbands*[1] Vikki Stark speaks of women who have been left all of a sudden. What she says would definitely work for men too, because pain and grief are truly genderless. She too identifies several stages to the process, from the announcement that your partner is no longer wishing to stay with you, all the way to recovery. She uses analogies, ranging from the 'tsunami' of the discovery of the betrayal to the 'summer day' of the recovery and going through 'thunderstorm', 'ice storm' and 'fog'. Her words ring true and it can be very helpful to realise that suffering is a normal occurrence in the circumstances and that it eases with time.

What matters here is to realise that as time goes on your emotions will evolve. It is impossible to give a timescale for this to happen because all individuals are different. But I can say categorically that eventually you will begin to heal and slowly start to create a new life which you will enjoy.

You may find it reassuring to know that you are not alone going through such a traumatic event. Many people have experienced this and the effect it has on their emotions.

Although grief is complicated and convoluted, you will heal eventually. Recovery is not a straight line upwards; it goes through ups and downs, and sometimes you will feel that you are not making any progress at all. Be assured this is not the case. With help and support, you will make progress and you WILL definitely get better. Knowing this may help bring some normality into your life, where at present nothing feels normal.

I would like to share some advice which will help you feel better more quickly.

---

[1] Vikki Stark, *Runaway Husbands: The Abandoned Wife's Guide to Recovery and Renewal.* Green Light Press: 2010.

Don't try to make sense of the jilter's behaviour

As mentioned before, you may never understand why your partner has left. This is because you reason from your own perspective, and from where you stand, your partner's behaviour is completely bewildering.

What you need to realise is that their decision makes complete sense to them at the time. If they have decided to leave you for someone else, to them it is a fait accompli, and they will not be open to discussing it or giving you an explanation.

It is very difficult for an abandoned party to understand why their partner left, especially as at that time the jilter may be transmitting conflicting messages. For instance many people say to me that their partner was still making love with them until the very end. When you are left just after lovemaking, being dumped, let alone for someone else, is completely bewildering and a cruel blow.

You endlessly ask yourself the questions: Who was I married to? Was my marriage a sham? As can be seen in the following example:

> Sally is an attractive woman in her early 50s. Her husband left her for a younger woman. He was still making love to her regularly and in fact demanded a lot of sex until suddenly, out of the blue one morning, he told her he was leaving her. Sally was utterly devastated: in fact I have never seen anyone cry so much. She tortures herself trying to make sense of his behaviour but is not getting anywhere. She is feeling hurt and humiliated, and can't understand how he could have sex with her while seeing another woman.

Nothing around you seems normal and you are trying to make sense of the chaos that ensues. It feels like you are living a nightmare and that soon you will wake up and all will be back to normal. At this point in the breakup, you may be hoping that your partner will 'see sense' and come back to you. You rehearse what you would say and imagine wild scenarios of tearful reconciliation.

Yet the jilter is very unlikely to change his or her mind; they are just not coming back. However harsh it seems, you must learn to accept what is. You may never actually understand what happened, but it is important you accept it. It may go against the grain, but if you do not do that, you will waste time, energy and precious healing opportunities hoping for something that will ultimately fail.

When someone goes, it is their choice. By leaving, they have removed the possibility of 'working' at improving the relationship and of making things right. This is actually what hurts you most, as you feel that you were never given the opportunity to rescue the relationship. Some people do not want to give their partner the chance to discuss resolving the problems, because they have already decided to move on no matter what.

Do not waste energy thinking of the 'whys?' You can only start healing when you have accepted the new reality.

Instead: concentrate on yourself and how to move forward and start building a new life.

Start taking some control back

As you are going through the flood of emotions that the aftermath of a breakup brings, it is easy to think that you have lost all control of your life and that other people, partner, children, lawyers, are calling all the shots. It can feel like you have lost your compass and are drifting rudderless without clear direction.

Enough!

It is time to take some control back. This can be achieved by making some changes in your life. Initially the changes may be small: eating foods your partner did not like, driving home a different way, watching DVDs they would have disliked. What is important here is to do things that you did not do when they were around. Do something new, however small a step that feels. As time goes on the changes will be bigger and more significant.

> Josie: 'After M. finally cleared out, one day I sat in "his" armchair.
> Suddenly I saw our living room from a new angle. I was in charge.
> It felt good.'

This is a good example because not only is it a new step, albeit apparently small, but is 'daring' and certainly challenges the former status quo. For Josie it felt like a small victory, because she began to realise at that point that she would survive and be OK.

Aim at making at least one change a day. Make sure that the level of challenge increases with time. The bigger the challenge, the bigger your sense of achievement.

Challenging yourself is good on several levels. It takes you out of your comfort zone; it also shows you that you are capable of achieving something by yourself, and it makes you feel independent and more in charge of your life. When your partner goes, your confidence is shattered. It is absolutely vital to work on rebuilding it. Challenging yourself is a way of rebuilding a fragile confidence.

> Hayley is a civil servant who has been left by her husband. He sent a text message to inform her that the marriage was over. Not surprisingly she is angry and upset. He has moved straight in with a new woman and Hayley feels very rejected. Her daughter is fond of the new partner, who is establishing a good relationship with her. The little girl has a bedroom in the new house and has been given a puppy whom she adores. Although Hayley understands that her daughter is happy and does not see the new partner as a mum, she feels very threatened and completely out of her depth as a mother, let alone as a wife.

> During her marriage she had fallen into a rut, with a routine encompassing all aspects of their lives: same foods every week, same activities and frankly little space for fun. She spends a great deal of time cleaning and is very house-proud. She tells me that she has no friends. Her husband probably became very bored and frustrated with their life; he seems very happy in the new relationship. He is a good father.

Hayley feels safe with her rigid routine – it gives her a measure of control – and even more so now that everything else in her life seems to be on quicksand. Yet, such a regimented life is an unhealthy form of control. Her daughter keeps saying how much fun she has in her dad's new household, which is much more relaxed.

As we started to work together, I asked her to change something in her routine every day, such as varying the weekly menu and her route to work. Even at this level, the changes were a challenge for her; she cried when I asked her to do these things, but I remained adamant. With time, the challenges I set her became more and more significant: finding a new activity (she joined a running group), speaking to the shopkeepers in the village. She started to enjoy the tasks. She realised that she was beginning to have some fun. Then we worked at forging good memories for her daughter; activities they could do together which do not require money. Hayley threw herself into this challenge and tells me of having real giggles with her daughter. Now she feels much less threatened by the new woman in her husband's life.

It is important to challenge yourself on a deeper level as you are making progress. This is an essential part of the process taking you to a sustained recovery; and of course, you never know where this is going to take you.

I had a really good marriage and my partner left

On the whole, you may have thought that you had a reasonably good marriage, but was that really the case? All marriages have their ups and downs but it is a fact that some get to a point where they slowly deteriorate. This is a gradual process, and routine may dull your emotions, so it is not always obvious that things are going from bad to worse. You have been building on the positive and ignoring the not so good for so long. In fact you may know nothing else, and think that this is what life has dealt you, so you must just get on with it.

You are convinced that your marriage will last forever; however, when you scratch the surface, the picture is not as perfect as you imagined it was. Inevitably you start to realise you have been glossing over the cracks, probably for fear of rocking the boat. In the case of an affair, you may deep down have sensed that something was not right, but you did not quite get to the truth. It is a fact that people put up with poor relationships, as they are their normality, and can't imagine life without their partner. They settle for the status quo and ignore that they deserve or could have a better life.

> Bea is a successful lawyer, and so is her husband. She was utterly devastated by her husband's disappearance (he never told her that he was leaving and just went while she was at work). Her world was turned upside down and she was prepared to do anything to get him back. She was constantly texting, calling and emailing him, begging him to come back.
>
> The result was to make him more distant, and in fact he was using these outpourings against her. He had all the power.
>
> When I asked when was the last time that he had complimented her, hugged her, spoken to her apart from dealing with practical day to day routine, taken an interest in her life, she was shocked to find that she could not remember.

In a long marriage, it is easy to fall into a routine and to take each other for granted, which is a toxic pattern. Both women and men fundamentally need to feel that they are valued and appreciated. To preserve any relationship, people need to show and feel respect and regard. Sometimes 'taking for granted' becomes contempt and this is really dangerous – the put downs, the 'stonewalling' (the silent treatment), the meanness are all very corrosive.

Too many people settle for the mundane and do not get the fulfilment they deserve from a relationship. Often they 'walk on eggshells' or put up with a domineering partner because they do not want to create problems. Anything for a quiet life.

Remember that you are a person in your own right and fully deserving of a relationship which fulfils your needs as well as your partner's. A successful relationship is where partners have a mutual respect for each other and where neither party takes the other for granted.

Don't blame yourself

You keep asking yourself: 'What have I done wrong?'

In the immediate aftermath of the breakup, it is all too easy for the person who has been left to blame themselves. It is often the case that they feel responsible for everything that has gone wrong, are ashamed the marriage has broken down, and cannot face family or friends. They fill their head with all sorts of thoughts: 'I was not good enough, I should have been more attentive, I let myself go, I concentrated on the children, I worked too hard' etc.

Of course there may be some truth in all of this, but I always say to my clients that the breakup has probably little to do with what they have done or not done, said or not said.

Most marriages break down over a long period of time, rather than as a result of a sudden or isolated event. This is crucial: in reality, when this point is reached it is probably too late to save a relationship.

> Faye is a warm and vivacious church worker, and so is her husband. He left her after over 30 years of marriage where they had both enjoyed a busy life, sharing the responsibility of pastoral work and helping others. With the job comes a home. When her husband dumped her, he asked her to leave the house because the house

formed part of his job package. She had nowhere to go and no money. Instead of helping her with practical steps, he refused to communicate with her in any shape or form. He does not take her calls, does not answer her emails and refuses to see her. His brutal rejection is bewildering and incredibly hurtful.

In the haze Faye does not see that her husband's lack of communication may be a clear sign that he is feeling guilty. The truth is that he would rather not look at what he has done. He prefers evading reality. By doing so he does not have to face the consequences of his action.

In many cases the innocent party is blamed by the jilter for all that has gone wrong and made to feel guilty: 'it is your fault that I no longer love you; in fact I never really did'. How convenient for the jilter to say very hurtful things; it saves them from looking at their own role in the breakup. Typically they adopt a persona, an image where they look good. This is what they portray to the outside world and it makes it easier for them to deal with the situation and 'justify' the breakup.

Your 'rival'

Do not focus your thoughts and energy on that person; if you do, you give them all the power, and they seem huge in your mind, making you feel inadequate and sad.

The truth is they do not have that power unless you give it to them. Don't waste your energy on them, which only conjures up negative thoughts.

Instead:

- When thinking about the 'rival' becomes overwhelming, think of a sentence or a picture to bring them down to size in your mind. If this takes the form of expletives, so be it
- Maybe the 'rival' does not even want power over you. The new partner might well be struggling with their own guilt to some extent. They are probably not sitting with your ex-partner laughing about you every night. Like everyone else, they are getting on with their lives
- Work hard at keeping positive. Focus your energy on what you want, not on what you don't have.

One day you will realise that your rival is welcome to your former partner. You deserve so much better than someone who betrayed you, and you are moving on to much better things!

Separate facts from fiction

When your world is upside down and no good news is forthcoming, it is all too easy to imagine the worst and let your imagination run riot: 'What if I'm left with nothing, lose the house, am destitute or can't see my children, what if what if?' You imagine catastrophic scenarios, especially when you are lying awake in the middle of the night.

The first thing to realise is that feeling like this is normal. Take the time to let things settle and for your head to clear before making **ANY** decisions. Your fears are often compounded by your partner, who knows what buttons to press to upset you and make you feel vulnerable. Don't listen to their threats.

Remember:

- Just because your partner says something, it doesn't mean that it is true
- The vast majority of people's worries are about things that do not actually happen in the end. In other words, you are worrying about things which might not or will not happen
- In the light of day it is wise to ignore any thoughts you have between midnight and 6 am after yet another sleepless night. They are rarely sound
- Each time you worry, ask yourself: does this stand up to scrutiny?
- STICK TO THE FACTS – Is this actually true? Do I know this or do I imagine it?
- Do not waste energy worrying about what you cannot change
- Take steps to be proactive and regain control. For instance, get all the information you need to help you make informed decisions. This may include legal advice.

5

First things first:

FINDING SOME RELIEF

Sometimes, the best thing you can do is not think, not wonder, not imagine, not obsess. Just breathe and have faith that everything will work out for the best.

You are going through life-changing emotions.

When everything is bleak, the following are well-practised tips designed to help you through the initial shock and depth of despair.

First, a very difficult step: stop contacting them

DO NOT ring, text or email your partner. Don't ask friends about them. Do not follow their activities on social media.

Talking to an estranged partner when you are not emotionally ready serves no useful purpose and only makes things worse. In fact what you say could be used against you later, and you are very vulnerable at this stage.

I mentioned before that when we are in a relationship we adapt our personality to better fit with our partner. Consequently breaking up is immensely difficult to do. Even when parting from an abusive situation, people may experience temporary pangs of wanting to get back together and be part of a couple again.

Breaking up can feel like withdrawing from an addiction. After all, you spoke every day, you may have texted each other during the day, you were together all the time, and abruptly it has to stop. The withdrawal symptoms are overwhelming; everything reminds you of them. You find yourself desperate to ring or text them, to hear their voice. Yet you **must not**. An analogy would be that if you are addicted to alcohol, drinking is not a good idea.

Not contacting them can be very painful, but it is absolutely essential in order to start the recovery process.

Instead:

- Phone a friend who will listen to you, write a letter that you will not send. Wait for the need or panic to pass – it will.

Change the jilter's name on your mobile phone

You are likely to go in a panic mode when you see your partner's name on your mobile phone screen.

Changing their name means that when they ring you, it will give you a moment to pause and breathe. A way of regaining some control for yourself. You need to make them feel smaller in your mind.

Replace their name with something like:

- Think first
- Take a deep breath
- Complication.

Remove photos and screensavers showing the two of you smiling and in love. It only makes you feel more rejected and miserable.

Start taking some control back

Do something different to change your routine. This will help change your thought pattern. Do at least one new thing a day, however small it may seem at first. For example:

- Say 'hello' to someone you wouldn't normally talk to
- Eat a new foodstuff
- Do some physical activity
- Do some DIY
- Write out your feelings.

Think about having some fun. You have to come up with one enjoyable thing to do every day of your diary for the next week. Write it and do it!

Reconnect with who you really are

Breaking up may mean that you no longer know how to exist when you are not in a couple. You were used to being part of a couple, of a marriage, and suddenly it is over. You may experience a sense of loss of identity altogether. This is completely normal.

What are your answers to the fundamental questions: 'Who am I?' 'Who are my friends?' 'What do I enjoy?'

It is really important to get to know yourself again, so think about your answers to these questions. This will help you feel more comfortable being on your own. Only then will you be able to start feeling better.

Be kind to yourself

This may mean simply pampering yourself a little:

- have a massage
- get a manicure
- go for a walk
- go out to watch a film rather than doing the housework.

Be patient; do not expect to feel better too quickly.

Take the time you need.

Accept that pain needs to be worked through. Let yourself be with the pain of your loss. I call it 'licking your wounds' and staying in the harbour, out of the storm in order to mend your sails. Accept the pain. There is no magic wand, but with time and a few techniques it will get easier. Don't expect instant results.

If you have a bad day, don't think that you are pathetic, or going back to square one; you are just having a bad day. With time, there will be fewer bad days. Take it one step at a time – one hour at a time.

You are grieving, you are dealing with rejection.

Be gentle and compassionate with yourself.

Keep in touch with your friends

They are central to your recovery (and do not forget them when things improve for you). Research shows that our friends are an essential ingredient to our happiness, at all times. Maybe you have neglected them when you were in a relationship. Time to get back in touch.

You will also realise that it is at times of need that you get to know who your friends really are. Sometimes, they are not the ones you thought would be there for you. You will be hurt by 'friends' who are no longer around for you. These were only 'fair weather friends'. It hurts, but you have to let go.

You will also find support from people you do not expect. New friendships will be formed. Value them.

Say yes to all invitations. You need to change your daily routine and enjoy time out, away from the TV. It is nice to have an occasion to make an effort and dress up, and you never know where that might lead you.

Of course, being with friends and family is not the same as being in an intimate relationship, but these connections and keeping busy help the pain caused by rejection.

Focus on what you enjoy and force yourself to get out of the house

This is essential, and need not cost much. Of course, it is wonderful to plan a holiday, go on a spa break or buy new clothes if you can afford it. However, very small pleasures help too.

In particular, remember what you enjoyed doing when you were single, or when you were a teenager? Do you want to learn a new skill? Join a club? A walk in the park costs nothing, and neither does phoning a friend to have a moan and a giggle.

As time goes on you will be surprised to see that doing something nice, especially with other people, will take your mind off the breakup.

Also, this is the time to:

- Go outside, exercise and breathe fresh air; this will boost your endorphin levels
- Depending where you live, walking by the side of water is very calming

- Enjoy nature, observe the daily changes
- Listen carefully to the sounds around you
- Savour.

Get medical help

It is likely that your eating and sleeping patterns have become erratic. In order to function, you need to sleep and feel calmer. Go and see your GP, who may prescribe medication for the short term. You might also need to be signed off work for a while. Alternatively consult a therapist such as a herbalist who can also help you.

See a professional

Yes, as a relationship coach, I would say that, but seeing an experienced professional will help speed up the recovery process. A good relationship specialist will give you unconditional support and empathy. More importantly, they will also ask difficult questions to get you unstuck from the misery. They will make you see that you are not guilty of being a bad and unlovable person. You will also understand that what you are going through is not unique and that you are not alone. A specialist will also give you tips and strategies to cope with the pain and then to move on.

6
Towards a deep shift in your mindset

When something bad happens, you have three choices:
Let it define you, let it destroy you or let it strengthen you.

A life-changing event

A breakup is life-changing. Everything you had taken for granted in your marriage and indeed your life as you know it has come to an end. It overturns all that is familiar, including any hopes and dreams you had for the future. Just at the point in your life when you may have been looking forward to some quality time with your partner, they leave. For whatever reason (which you may never fully understand) they do not want to spend that time with you.

> Laura's children have left home. She is excited for her future and sees this time as the ideal opportunity to rekindle her marriage and spend quality and carefree time with her husband. She decides to retire early and focus on being with her partner and make plans about holidays and travel with him. Unexpectedly and without warning he leaves her. She therefore finds herself alone, no children still at home, nowhere to live and, having given up her job, no source of income. So from being very happy and looking forward to the future, she finds she has lost everything.

With such a devastating event, it is hardly surprising people find themselves facing an unknown future, not knowing how they will cope. Initially this leaves them with an all-consuming feeling of total rejection. In actual fact, this is a turning point in their life, and with support they will come to realise they have an opportunity to build a better future for themselves.

Stay in the 'not-knowing'

When faced with life-changing events, you understandably feel bewildered and confused. The shock is often so great that you cannot think straight. You analyse the situation, you go over and over the same ground, you relive the conversations you have had before and during the breakup, you blame yourself, you imagine wild scenarios of reconciliation. Basically, you drive yourself almost crazy with uncertainty and indecisiveness.

As a result, you no longer know where you stand, and you are certainly not in the right frame of mind for making difficult decisions.

Stop!

Instead:

Stay in the not-knowing. This means:

- Determine that you will not decide anything until a certain date. Give yourself a few weeks to make decisions. Bear the date in mind. Until then, do not decide anything
- When the questions come to your mind, just say to yourself: 'I will decide on such a date. In the meantime, I am staying with the not-knowing'
- Just be
- Think of something else
- This will give you much-needed space and time.

When you no longer torture yourself and let the dust settle, the answers will come to you.

So when you start going round in circles again, stop. You are not required to find a solution yet. Relax. Wait. Sit still.

Do not push anything. Do not force anything. Do not attempt to persuade anyone. The answers will come to you, and they will be right for you.

Your partner is not coming back.

In my experience it is totally natural for people to want everything to go back to how it was before, when everything appeared to be lovely and everyone was happy, at least that is how you see it. But as you have reached this stage, there were probably issues that were not being addressed that have brought you to this point. In some cases it is people's first thought to try and resolve these problems to keep the marriage going, and may even invent scenarios whereby the jilter realises the error of their ways and comes back begging for forgiveness. You need to accept that this is not going to happen.

> Tina is a particularly lovely woman who has been left without any form of explanation, and this has left her feeling completely devastated. Over the weeks, I have worked with her at accepting her situation; she is having difficulty understanding how she has reached this point and why her partner has left her. She feels guilty at not being able to provide a stable family unit for her children. She is also upset by the ripple effect that separation after a long marriage entails – she could lose contact with her extended family, including her in-laws whom she got on well with.

> With my support she has now reached the stage where she is ready to start building a better future for herself. At our third session, what struck me most was that she had removed her wedding, engagement and eternity rings. She tells me that she has finally realised that her husband is not coming back. Moreover, she says she no longer wants him back, because she does not like the selfish person he has become.

> This is a momentous step forward for her. I tell her that it is still good to cherish the happy memories from their time together, but that she is making a very positive step towards starting a new phase in her life.

> She has taken control of her situation and is initiating the divorce. Even though her husband is now dragging his heels, this has not prevented Tina from moving forward with her life.

Once you have taken back control for your own decisions, you start to regain a sense of self-esteem. This will help you to see and acknowledge your partner's flaws and hopefully why you no longer want the jilter back.

Relationships are based on trust. You realise that your partner has broken that trust by their actions, making it very difficult to rebuild what you had together. After so much betrayal, there is no going back.

Do not appear needy

How will you seem if you are looking helpless and pathetic when your former partner is already detached from you? Be honest with yourself: will it make things better, or worse?

Instead:

For your own sake and self-esteem, stop begging your partner to come back. You are not a doormat. And how much better will you feel when you maintain your dignity and the moral high ground?

- Learn to laugh again
- Practise laughing and smiling in front of the mirror. It may sound a bit weird, but actually it appears to give the instinctive part of your brain the message that you are happy
- Keep your head held high and shoulders back (you can cry later, but never in front of the jilter)
- Work on your self-esteem; you are a worthy human being
- Keep your pride intact (no begging). You deserve better.

Learn to let go

Learning to let go and get over what has just happened to you will take time. In its own way a marriage breakup feels like a bereavement. Arguably it is worse than a bereavement at first, because on top of the emptiness and shock, you have to deal with other emotions such as jealousy and rejection. However, as time passes you will realise that better times are ahead and that one day you will feel much better.

At any rate, being dumped comes as a shock, and you need time to adjust to life without your partner. There will be lots of different feelings and emotions running through your head, making it difficult to move on. You may feel angry with the injustice of it all and wonder what you have done to deserve this. This is normal, and is just one of the stages you will go through to rebuild your life. Don't rush this stage: remember that you need time to lick your wounds before you can move on. There is a time for tears and for feeling sorry for yourself – that is normal and healthy – but this will pass.

Sooner rather than later, you will realise that remaining stuck in the negative or clinging to fantasy is not getting you anywhere. Besides, you have probably shed enough tears. A client said to me that she had reached the stage where she was bored of listening to herself and was wondering what effect she had on her friends! Yet I know of people who are still stuck in the misery 10, 20 years later. What a pitiful life.

Eventually you come to realise that your estranged partner has moved on and you can do the same. Ask yourself, is it helpful for you to be continuously looking back and using negative energy? That will not change what has happened, it will only prevent you moving forward.

When you are feeling stronger, you will come to accept that the person you used to love no longer exists. Enough is enough. This is the time when your emotions begin to shift: instead of moping and looking back, you will start to realise it is time to take control and start rebuilding your life.

Don't be a 'doormat'

A doormat is someone who systematically ignores his/her own needs. Being a doormat is certainly not the way to emerge from a bad situation.

A doormat listens to their partner's demands and says: 'I have to do this'; 'I should do this'. In other words, you ignore your own needs and take on the role imposed by your partner. As a result, you constantly 'tread on eggshells':

- You try to second guess what your partner wants
- You reach a point where you forget what your own needs are
- You even forget who you really are.

Some people who have been left by a partner wrongly assume that if they were more like the person their partner wanted then they would not have been left. Nothing is further from the truth. It's not about you; it's all about control.

> No one likes or respects a doormat – least of all you! How does it make *you* feel?
>
> I can assure you that your partner would have left no matter what.

Instead:

Work hard at rediscovering who you are: your needs, wants, strengths, values etc.

This book will help you.

7
Getting divorced

You cannot rewrite the past – only lay down plans for the future.

You may find that your estranged partner is asking you to initiate divorce proceedings, although this is the last thing you want to do at this stage. You may even find yourself going down that route when inside you are very reluctant to go ahead. After all, it is not you who wants any of this.

Only initiate proceedings if it is what you really want to do.

Do not be coerced into it, especially when your emotions are still raw. I have seen many cases of clients being asked to initiate the divorce. Suggesting divorce is yet another way for the estranged partner to wield power and to test boundaries. They often say that they are just trying 'to save you the pain of reading bad things about yourself'. In reality, they are aware that they cannot come up with sensible reasons for justifying the divorce. Whereas you could use reasons such as unreasonable behaviour or adultery, the jilter is not keen to have to find reasons why he/she should divorce you.

> Nevertheless it is best to get advice at an early stage even if you do not feel ready to divorce. Sometimes there may be legal reasons/ advantages to divorcing at an early stage and it is important to be in receipt of all the facts before deciding whether or not to wait.

Interestingly, you may find that once you initiate divorce proceedings, the jilter backs off, because they have lost control over the situation. At this point, you will realise whether or not *you* want to go ahead with the divorce.

Remember also that, however amicable, it will certainly be difficult to read divorce papers. You are likely to read things about you that are unpleasant. So, do not do anything until you are ready to sever all links. In my experience that takes time, and until you want to date and remarry in the future, there is no rush. If the jilter is in a new relationship, their new partner may be putting them under pressure to get divorced quickly. That is their problem, not yours.

Make decisions for you and your future when you feel ready to make them, and only then. Equally if you feel that you have nothing to gain by remaining married, then so be it. At the very least, make an informed choice: find out where you stand and what your rights are.

When you are ready to get divorced, **it is imperative that you seek legal advice.**

There is only one basic ground for divorce in the UK: 'irretrievable breakdown of the marriage'. This has to be proved by evidence of one of the following:

- Adultery
- Unreasonable behaviour
- Desertion
- Two years' separation (only with the consent of the other party)
- Five years' separation (with or without the consent of the other party).

In practice, most couples opt for 'unreasonable behaviour' as the stated grounds for the divorce.

It is essential that you get proper legal advice at this stage. Not only must you be clear of what your rights are, but this is an excellent way of exercising real control over the situation. Taking the initiative can be a very cathartic development for you.

Be wary of husbands/wives claiming that things will remain amicable. Often their intentions are questionable. Even if they are sincere, things can and do go wrong at a later date. Disagreements over assets, possessions, children, money, can arise at any point in the proceedings.

I have had many clients, women and men, who have been discouraged from being properly represented because the partner had claimed that the divorce could be straightforward. Even if the divorce is indeed amicable (for example if you agree on the division of the assets or the children are grown up), you need individual legal advice. I can understand that more and more couples decide to represent themselves to save money; but this may end up being an expensive mistake. A divorce after a long marriage is a huge step.

Be aware that as a married person you are entitled to a settlement which is fair and equitable. I have worked with many married clients who had stayed in a bad relationship for fear of ending up destitute, because that is what their spouse had told them would happen. That would not be the case. If there is a house, a pension, some equity, then you are entitled to a share.

It is worth investigating 'softer' options leading to a resolution outside the Courts.

For instance:

- Mediation: mediators help you and your partner work through issues in order to find a solution. The agreed outcome can be checked by family solicitors
- Collaborative Law: you, your partner and both lawyers sit round a table to reach an agreement.

There are other options which you should discuss with your legal adviser.

If you cannot reach an agreement, you may be in a more adversarial situation which may ultimately lead to Court proceedings.

If you have been cohabiting for a long time rather than being legally married, matters are different. My understanding is that your rights are much less clear cut and that there is no such thing as a 'common-law husband or wife'. You will need very good legal advice.

What matters is that you:

- take control of your decisions
- make informed choices
- get what you are entitled to.

8
Beware of self-destructive behaviours

Life is too short to argue and fight with the past.
Count your blessings, value your loved ones and
move on with your head held high.

When you feel deeply betrayed and hurt, it is natural to have unkind thoughts towards your partner. With time, however, you have to change your mindset and learn to channel your energies into recovering with the aim of moving forward. Start by appreciating what you have rather than yearning for what you no longer have.

Occasionally, some people seem to remain stuck in the anger phase. They cannot move on. They simply do not see that their actions are damaging to themselves rather than their former partner.

A few words of advice.

Do not be bitter and jealous

Kate is a successful businesswoman in her late 50s. She and her husband built up a company which employs them both. Now they have over 100 employees. As the company became more successful, they kept moving to better, larger houses. Eventually they moved to a farmhouse that they renovated at great expense. As builders were in the house for over two years, life was chaotic and Kate became exhausted and very resentful. Her husband would turn up late at night, expecting to be fed in an immaculate house with the large dogs walked, washed, and groomed. Kate pretty much ran herself to the ground trying to do it all. She started to complain and moan, feeling increasingly resentful. One day she realised that they had not had sex for two years.

He moved out and found another (younger) woman with whom he moved in. Two years later, Kate has no other focus in her life and no other conversation than speaking of him and his new partner. She is acting compulsively: she checks his email and bills (she knows how much he spends every month on restaurants, hotels and holidays), she speaks to him every day, texts him constantly on the slightest pretext, speaks to shopkeepers where he has shopped, expects birthday gifts, makes fun of the new girlfriend's children, resents their lifestyle. She is envious of their new home. She is obsessed and sounds very bitter.

The result is not surprising: her acquaintances and friends have deserted her and she is losing the respect of her colleagues. She is in fact being ostracised as a company director and many decisions are made without consulting her, which incenses her. She is incandescent with rage and consumed by bitterness. Her blood pressure is off the scale and her doctor is concerned. Her lawyer is frustrated by her refusal to finalise the divorce (she constantly introduces new obstacles). Her legal fees are mounting.

If there is an example of how not to do a breakup, this is it!

Sadly Kate refuses to move on from her self-destructive mindset and does not see that by doing that she is poisoning her own life, while her husband and his new partner are living the high life, spending money and having a fantastic time.

If you keep dwelling on the jilter's new relationship – which has nothing to do with you – then the other party wins in every way.

Remember the adage: 'What you resist persists!'

Instead:

- Stop obsessing. The more you focus on your rival, the more they are the centre of your life, and the less you will move on
- Work on the positive
- Start focusing on your own life. What do you want it to look like in the future?
- Start reinventing a new you
- Using the advice in this book will definitely help you.

Cut your losses

Financial loss forms part of a relationship breakup. A breakup can be expensive for all parties.

- Sometimes you have to accept that losing money is part of the situation. It may hurt and feel unfair, but neither breakups, nor life itself, are fair. This is just the way it is.

You may lose friendships too. Some friends are torn and do not know how to deal with your new situation. They are taking sides. This is very hurtful, but do not dwell on negative emotions. You will make new friends in your new life.

Instead:

- Try not to force friends to take sides by continually criticising the jilter to them or endlessly getting them to report back to you about his/her latest actions or behaviour
- Keep to the moral high ground: do not spread rumours, and if you hear false rumours about yourself, just say that what you hear is simply not true. No further detail is required. A divorce should not be a matter for gossip
- Realise that through this you are really understanding who your real friends are. Some people will be extremely supportive. These are your real friends.

Avoid thoughts of revenge

Just as jealousy is destructive to you, so is revenge. Negative emotions are more likely to destroy you than the jilter.

Instead:

- Start focusing on you, what matters most, and what you want your life to look like
- Enjoy rediscovering who you really are and become your own best friend.

Do not attempt to turn the children against your former partner

You may be tempted to vent your frustrations and to offload onto the children. A lot of the time your views of your partner's behaviour may be entirely justified, but you must not involve your children. The breakup is yours, not theirs.

> Alice is a proud housewife. She and her husband started going out together as young teenagers. She worked very hard to support her husband while he built up their businesses. They lived frugally until the businesses became very successful and now own a huge house surrounded by a massive walled garden, land and woods.
>
> During her marriage, Alice saw her role, in fact her vocation, as keeping the house, raising the children and making everything easy for her husband when he came home. After the children left the family home, her husband suddenly announced that he was leaving her. He moved in with a much younger career woman and shares with her a lifestyle of work and glamorous holiday breaks.
>
> Alice is angry and bewildered. She cries constantly. Even four years on, she still cries all the time. She never speaks to anyone directly. She asks her elder son to make all her calls and never answers her phone. She has no mobile and no email, so she is not contactable. She has isolated herself and has stopped seeing other people. She remains on her own in her huge house and refuses to sell and downsize. She has fallen out with all her friends. All communication is done through her children, who are now adults with their own lives to live. They all actually work in the family business, in other words for their father.
>
> All have wives and children, but everyone is expected to drop everything when she calls 'family council meetings' round the kitchen table. The children have to attend and must support her views. She even invited her husband to talk over dinner, but when he turned up he realised that he was actually being trapped by her and their three children ganging up against him. This happened twice, and each time degenerated into a slanging match between the parents in front of the children and even grandchildren.

It does not occur to Alice that she is forcing her children to take sides and does not give them any choice as to which side that should be. She does not realise how manipulative she is, nor what a risk she takes if any of her children rebel and blame her later for not keeping communication channels open for their dad.

The root of Alice's behaviour is that while she remains needy, her children constantly run after her. Her anger towards her husband is so severe that she wants the children to cut themselves from him and side with her, at any price.

Do not use your children as pawns or messengers. Do not make them take sides, no matter how you feel about their other parent. This applies to children of all ages, including adult children. They have their own unique relationship with the other parent, and should be allowed to work through this for themselves.

Of course, it is fine to show sadness, but remember who the adult is and who the child is in this situation. A grown man or woman behaving like a spoilt little child does not attract any respect. All they do is risk damaging their children and their relationship with their children.

> *Instead:*
>
> - Make sure that you try to speak of your former partner with respect
> - Rise above bad behaviour and do not descend to the jilter's level
> - Keep your own counsel
> - Facilitate access and contact (obviously this does not apply if there has been domestic or sexual abuse, or if you have definite knowledge that your children are frightened of the jilter or the jilter's new partner).

Your children ideally need input from both parents.

Do this for your children's benefit, even if it requires a huge effort from you.

Celebrate what was good

When things have gone wrong, it is all too easy to think that your marriage was a sham. You start imagining that you were deluded all along. You torture yourself wondering if the whole time together was a waste of your time and energy. Well it was not.

Remember how it was while it was good. Look at the positive consequences: you may have children for instance, or a successful joint business, and definitely special memories too. Do not discard them. Instead, treasure them. You did not imagine those times. They were real. This will help you realise that you are not a failure. You loved, and were loved, and then your relationship ended. It is simply a fact that some relationships run their course.

The victim mentality

Some people remain tortured a very long time after the breakup of their relationship. They are stuck in what is called the 'victim mentality' trap. That is their mindset and where they choose to stay.

They identify with the traumatic event, like being dumped, to the point that they see it as something which defines them as a person.

Somehow they think that by behaving that way they will appeal to the jilter. They try to make him/her feel guilty. Of course this does not work.

In contrast, a healthy mindset will help you work through the trauma, and not let it define you. You will eventually see these crises as opportunities to grow.

Self-destructive behaviours:

- Do not solve anything
- Do not make your former partner love you
- Do not make you an attractive person to be around
- *Do* make you lose your sense of self-worth. You let yourself down.

9

Affairs:

'I HAVE LOST MY PAST, MY FUTURE'

'No one can make you feel inferior without your consent.'
Attributed to Eleanor Roosevelt

Often, my clients have to deal with their partner's affair and that is a tough ordeal.

There is no gentle way of saying this. The truth is that most people leave because there is another person involved. Very few people leave a long-established relationship to be on their own. Most of the time they leave to be with another person, or at least because another person has been a catalyst for change. Many partners who stray deny it initially or forever, but a third party is often the reason for their departure. They often claim that they need space and time on their own, which is almost a giveaway that this stage announces the end of the relationship. However they still deny the truth and even accuse their faithful partner of questioning and intimidating them. The result is that you often end up feeling guilty that you don't believe them. No wonder that you are so confused. As for the jilter, once a lie is told it becomes easier and lies just roll off the tongue.

It is hard to describe how it feels to be left for someone else and lied to in the process. Saying that you are feeling deeply humiliated and betrayed is an understatement. Not only is your relationship over, you have lost all you know, your life is turned upside down, but you have to deal with overwhelming emotions such as humiliation and jealousy. You start to think that you will never trust anyone again. To top it all, you feel taken for a fool. Often also you are left guessing.

Affairs bring chaos because they affect many people, not just the partner who has been betrayed. Affairs have ramifications for children, family, and friends as well.

Why do people have affairs?

There are many reasons why people have affairs. All relationships are individual. However, in my experience, the reasons are one or more of the following:

- The partner who strays wants to try something new
- They feel stuck in a rut
- They wonder if there is more to life
- They are susceptible to flattery and attention
- They are bored with their existing relationship and believe that the grass is greener elsewhere
- They do not think that the affair will be discovered
- They feel that they can re-live the excitement of their youth
- They enjoy the chase and the element of novelty
- They think that it will not change anything in their current relationship; they 'want to have their cake and eat it'
- They do not truly think of the consequences of their actions, and this only gets worse the longer the deceit goes on
- They are going through personal or professional problems but do not want to face them, so the affair is a form of escapism
- They are worried about ageing
- They no longer communicate with their partner
- An opportunity occurred and they went along with it.

Can a relationship survive an affair?

It rarely can. Affairs are devastating and create chaos and destruction. This is because relationships are based on trust and mutual respect, both of which are completely destroyed when one party has an affair. For this reason, I tend to think that a relationship never gets back to what it was after an affair. Partners may be able to live with each other but the relationship may never be the same again.

Occasionally, when the straying partner sees the devastation the process of splitting up entails, they endeavour to salvage the relationship.

Should you ever take your partner back?

At the beginning, you may want your partner back at all costs.

- You may be clinging to hope
- You may have young children and cannot face giving them a future in a single parent household

- You may believe that you have invested so much in a long relationship that you are not prepared to give up
- You feel that there is too much at stake
- You wonder if you have really tried hard enough to salvage the relationship
- Sometimes you feel so wretched on your own that you begin to wonder if you should give your estranged partner another chance.

Fear of being alone is a very powerful emotion. Society compounds the belief that we are whole only as part of a couple. We are programmed to be comfortable with what we know and fearful of trying something new. However, this does not make it a good reason to take a partner back.

Many prefer pretending that there is nothing wrong and that you can wallpaper over the cracks, believing that there is no good to come out of rocking the boat:

> Robin is a self-employed professional man in his 50s. He is gentle and kind. His wife left him for another man, although she never admitted that to him, but he knows what is happening. She prefers blaming him for the breakup, claiming that he is dull and boring.
>
> He is distraught and wants her back at all costs. He tells me that she had been unfaithful in the past but that he had taken her back. I asked how they had managed to overcome her infidelity in the past. He replied that he tried even harder to please her. When I asked what she did to fulfil her part of the bargain, he said 'nothing', and that they had not discussed it at the time.
>
> Clearly nothing had been resolved. The result was that the relationship endured for a while but the same problem re-emerged later. As a result, Robin has to go through heartache again, only this time it feels worse because he feels that all his effort and self-denial were a waste of time.

Rebuilding a relationship, and therefore trust, is difficult and requires patience and hard work. One client who did achieve it told me that it took a lot of 'sheer bloody-mindedness' to rebuild her marriage.

How to rebuild a relationship is not the purpose of this book, but when you are considering trying to save your marriage, you must:

- Take stock and acknowledge where you are and what has brought you to this point
- Gain clarity. In effect this is all about talking. Talk, communicate. Discuss how you got to that point. Everything needs to be in the open. Without that, there is no chance. If you want any future together, you must clear out the debris in order to rebuild solid foundations again
- Learn to function as a couple again: go on dates. Start a new activity together. Have fun
- Start communicating properly – and keep talking.

Taking a partner back and forgiving are very difficult things to do. Relationships are based on trust, so it is hard to see how any relationship can recover from such betrayal. However, on rare occasions, a partner is able to forgive and start again. If you make the decision to take your partner back and try again, you must both do so with a complete determination to forgive and move on.

Deciding to salvage the marriage or terminating it is very difficult.

- Take your time. Stay in the not-knowing for a while. Be honest. Do not allow others to influence your decision, one way or another
- Deciding to break up or not has to be right for YOU, strictly you and no one else, not even your children.

A thought: Life is about endings and new beginnings

One day, you may be surprised to realise that actually you no longer want your partner back. You realise that the relationship is truly over and that you deserve better. When this happens, it is a huge moment which really shows that the process of healing has started.

10
A brief word about the menopause

As this book is designed for people in their 40s and above, I find it necessary to mention a factor which affects women, of course, but also indirectly men, because they may be unprepared to deal with the symptoms of their partner's menopause.

The menopause can be very debilitating for some women. The symptoms can make a woman feel vulnerable and unattractive. They include:

- Hot flushes and night sweats
- Disturbed or sleepless nights, leading to tiredness, exhaustion, and even depression
- Difficulty in concentrating and thinking clearly, memory loss
- Weight gain and changes in the body
- Mood swings
- General aches and pains
- Headaches and migraines
- Loss of confidence and self-esteem
- Loss of sense of self.

The menopause is an obvious reminder that a woman is ageing, raising difficult questions about her identity and purpose: Who am I? What do I want? Am I past my best? Is it the slippery slope towards the end? Am I old? Will a man ever find me attractive again? Women in their 50s and 60s complain that they suddenly feel invisible.

In many ways the menopause is a reminder to men that they are ageing too. If their life partner has so clearly hit mid-life, may be even become a grandparent, then so have they. If a man chooses to leave his wife for a younger woman, it is hard to see him disposing of his past, and making a fool of himself in his wife's eyes. Being with an ageing woman reminds a man that he is ageing too. Being seen in the arms of a younger woman can be an ego booster, at least for a while.

I believe that mature women left by their partner, and especially if for a younger woman, precisely at the time when they are going through the upheaval of the menopause, endure a particularly painful time requiring specific mental resources.

When a man leaves his middle-aged wife for a younger woman it can seem to be the ultimate betrayal for her. Not only has her life been turned upside down and she experiences complete rejection, but a younger woman is enjoying what she thought was rightfully hers. Both parties have worked hard and sacrificed a lot in the process of building a marriage, a family, a home and sometimes a business.

To make matters worse, this is a time when the couple's children are leaving home. At that time, many people dream of rekindling passion in the marriage and enjoying more privacy. Their partner may have very different views. In the past, they used to confide in someone they saw as their soulmate. Following a breakup, they realise that they have lost that comfort too.

> One client, Justine, confided: *'One of the hardest things to bear was that the person I most wanted to confide in about the terrible thing that had happened was the very person who had caused the anguish.'*

When you were in your marriage, life was meaningful. You counted on your partner's love and support to help you through difficult times. The menopause was just another challenge in the course of a long marriage, which would be borne by both. Yet this is not to be – your partner has gone.

Men who leave a long marriage for a younger woman are often attempting to evade uncomfortable and mundane realities. It is a form of escapism. Their lifelong partners know them too well (the familiarity breeds contempt syndrome), whereas the younger woman might well be impressed by a lifestyle, a maturity.

> Norma is a bubbly woman in her early 50s who has adult daughters. Her husband left her out of the blue, although he had prepared his departure carefully. Norma returned home one evening to find her husband's shelves empty of clothes and belongings. He sent her a text informing her that he had left for good and that he was not coming back. Despite her questions, he refused to acknowledge why. She asked if he was seeing someone else and he denied this. She is tormented by his lack of communication. She later discovered that he is involved with a much younger woman, who has a successful career, no children and a very enviable lifestyle.

She found out that together they jet off for glamorous holidays and have bought a yacht, ideal for lavish parties. Sadly **Norma** knows that her husband's business is in trouble and she realises that his involvement with the other woman coincided with the company's downward slide.

Another repercussion of this is as their wife's fertility comes to an end, some men start new families at that stage. This is a very cruel blow for a mature woman who is no longer physically able to start or complete a family.

Jill had always wanted children, but her husband did not want to start a family. They were busy creating a very successful business and their lifestyle was luxurious: racehorses, exotic holidays and a beautiful country house. Each time Jill raised the subject of children, her husband gifted her a new dog. Her husband left her the day after her 60th birthday for a woman who had young children. He is so besotted with them that he and his new girlfriend are speaking of starting their own family. No wonder that Jill is feeling utterly betrayed and dejected.

There are few words of comfort in this situation. Getting a dog is an expedient solution and it also ties the person. A dog can be seen as a baby substitute, a toddler who never grows up. On some level this is a clever plan to avoid fatherhood with her. She grows to accept it, and her fertility declines with time.

It is a slap in the face to realise that, while your partner didn't want a child with you for all of your long marriage, he appears to be happy to take the plunge with someone he has only known for a short time. It is like a public statement that you were not good mother material. What is happening, of course, is that the jilter needs to prove that he is still virile at that late stage in life. Recovering from such a betrayal when it is too late to have a baby with someone else is probably the hardest thing of all for a woman to bear.

11
Discovering a better you

Surrender to what is, let go of what was,
and have faith in what will be. *Sonia Ricotti*

Betrayal and loss shake you to the very core, to the extent that you no longer know who you are or what to do with your life. You are reeling with grief, shock and a gamut of emotions. You do not recognise yourself.

Days have passed; you have cried, wept, screamed, paced the floor, and felt that you were in a bottomless pit of darkness. You know that this cannot go on: you have to try and find a way to survive.

Now it is time to start the healing process

However painful the process is, and it is, the very fact that you have to lay yourself bare emotionally, in order to go back to your core, to your deep values will help you find a new and better you. You will discover a new reason for being. When you manage to do this, you will realise that you have at long last turned a page.

Having 'de-selfed' and compromised your own value in order to feed your partner's over many years, this is undoubtedly time to reclaim who you were when you met and who deep down *you still are.*

Not only that, but a few years down the line, many women and men realise that in effect, their ex-partner did them a favour: they have had the opportunity to grow as a person, achieve things they never dreamt of before. They have opened their heart and mind to new experiences and new people.

Things don't have to change the world to be important. *Steve Jobs*

Take care of yourself

Losing weight, or more usually gaining weight, can happen at times of intense stress. Rather than dieting or making drastic changes to your lifestyle, it is better to think of **rebalancing your life,** and **eating a balanced and healthy diet.**

Think fit, rather than slim.

Nurture yourself and your body: be kind to yourself

You are probably mentally and physically exhausted. Severe stress and lack of sleep can take their toll on your wellbeing. You may be tempted to punish your body.

Instead:

- Be kind to yourself. Pamper yourself. Take a warm candle-lit bath – this will remind you that you are worthy
- Smell a flower, bake a cake, or book a massage, anything that will make you feel pampered and improve your mood and self-esteem
- If you are a woman, put your make up on – **this is an essential** – and wear clothes that make you feel good. If you are a man, shave and get dressed in smart clothes. If you were ever to bump into your partner, you must look good; this is a matter of self-pride. Chin up, head high and be in control of the situation. **Feeling good about yourself is very empowering**
- Take up gentle exercise, especially out of doors. The fresh air is excellent to clear the mind, and exercise releases endorphins, the 'feel good' hormones
- Watch alcohol. You may feel temporarily better if you drink because it anaesthetises the pain to some extent. However, the effect does not last, because alcohol produces only an artificial relief. Alcohol is also a depressant, which solves nothing at all. A glass of wine with friends is a good way to unwind, but a bottle on your own is not. Even if you find an excuse in your mind

for drinking, be aware of the risks to your health and wellbeing. While you are dulling the pain with alcohol, you are not taking any real steps to make things better

- Same with sugary foods. It's easy to finish the pack of biscuits that you had started. But putting on weight will only make you feel even more miserable, more worthless, and less attractive.

Later on, you may feel ready to:

- Start playing a sport, dancing, walking; anything you will enjoy
- These activities will take you out of yourself for a few hours
- You will also get fitter (maybe your former partner will see the new trimmer, healthier, happier you one day!)
- Additional benefit: you meet like-minded people. Suddenly, you have a new social circle.

Develop gratitude and a 'glass half full' attitude

Be grateful, even (especially) for little things. Research shows that gratitude is the most healthy feeling or frame of mind we can experience. Become mindful of the beauty of nature, of the kindness of strangers. Learn to appreciate the small things and to see their value in your quality of life.

- Think daily of the positive aspects of your life. What are they? What always makes you feel good?
- Recall the positive moments of your day: a beautiful sunset, a smile from a toddler, a phone call from a friend, the first daffodils in the park…
- Be grateful for the blessings you have. Say thank you. Express your gratitude, even if it is not directed at any specific entity
- Each night, recall and enter in your diary three things you are thankful for. Or try this:

I would send myself an email every night with the things from that day that I should be thankful for, and I would read it the next day. Sometime later, I realized that it's a very powerful form of psychological therapy. *Jose Luis Caceres, quoted in the Huffington Post*

Take up new activities and learn new skills

This will get you out of the house. Instead of feeling gloomy it will help you focus on positive developments. It will help you discover that you are worthy. Some examples:

- Making wellbeing a goal
- Going outside and walking in the fresh air
- Exercising at a gym
- Joining a sports club or a dancing class
- Eating healthily
- Ensuring that your social life gets more active
- Learning a new skill
- Travelling or at least going away for a weekend
- Volunteering for charity
- Joining an evening class. What about woodworking, upholstery, pottery, learning a musical instrument or a foreign language?
- Joining a book group
- Studying for a qualification
- Going back to university/University of the Third Age (U3A)
- Considering a change of career
- Planning a trip
- Moving house (not always a choice, but an opportunity to make the new place your own).

Discover who you are and what you are capable of. Keep an open mind and even take a risk! Not only will you learn new skills, which helps build your self-esteem, but again you are likely to meet like-minded people.

Learn to live alone and enjoy it

It can be very hard to find yourself alone, especially at weekends. Everyone you see appears to be living happily in a couple! Do not stay in moping in front of the TV though. Even if it feels like a huge effort, get out. Why not decide to say yes to any invitation coming your way? Simply get out of the house: you are free to do as you please. When did that last happen? You will be surprised to receive invitations from unexpected sources, such as colleagues, neighbours, and friends.

Say yes; open yourself to possibilities, even if it feels like one more ordeal to go through. At the very least, it is better than staying in watching TV. Besides, you will meet other people. That is fun and you do not know where it might take you. If it takes you to a date, then so be it. Meeting someone organically does happen.

On the other hand, some people find they are actually happier being on their own, at least some of the time:

> Sophie, who was left by her partner of 16 years: *'I actually had a whirlwind of activities during the first few weeks. My friends were keen to invite me to various events and at any rate I was on the lookout for new experiences. Doing this helped me get through the first few weeks.*
>
> *'However, I soon realised that I needed to enjoy my own space too and that my home was my cocoon. I needed to learn to enjoy pottering and being me, without the distraction of activities or other people. I discovered the joys of lounging in my comfy pyjamas too, and having little planned. This can be strangely comforting.'*

Clearly in this case Sophie is making a positive choice to stay in her pyjamas, unlike Megan, who was too depressed to get out of her dressing gown. Being comfortable on your own is so important for a successful recovery. Get out and be active, but at the same time, learn to enjoy your own company. One day, you will start relishing going home, closing the door and leaving the world behind. It can be comforting and peaceful.

Time to be you!

12
Dating again

*Be strong enough to let go, and patient enough
to wait for what you deserve.*

Open your heart, but best not to date straight away

Many dumped people feel the need to get straight back to the 'dating scene' if only to prove to their ex and indeed to themselves that they are still in demand and attractive to others.

I remember a client saying to me that she was going to (please forgive the language): 'shag her way out of this'. Although it may sound fun, this is definitely not a good idea, not least because it does not work. Immediately after a breakup, you are very vulnerable. You have to work through what happened, and come to terms with your own role in the breakup. You also have to learn lessons to ensure that you will not make the same mistakes again. At times of intense grief, you are not able to make good choices.

Actually a great number of books written with midlife or later years in mind simply give advice about dating in later life, implying that it is a must and a means to move on. They simply ignore the whole process of recovering from a breakup.

Recovering from the breakup, learning from it and finding a new form of happiness *outside of a relationship* are actually central to finding new intimate relationships in the future.

Online dating

*Don't try to rush things. Things will happen at the right time,
with the right person and for the best reason.*

If you are thinking of joining a dating website, remember that it is a double-edged sword. When you are left by someone, you have been seriously rejected, and rejection hurts, as you know only too well. Dating online may actually mean opening yourself to a huge amount of rejection. Yes, there are lots of positive stories about couples meeting their soulmate online and getting married, but there are many other accounts of people who are feeling like they have entered a 'meat market'. Some people keep 'butterflying' in the search for something constantly better. Others may even be pretending to be what they are not. Online dating can entail a more casual approach to meeting people and fails to address connecting on a deeper level. It is worth mentioning here that STDs are on the rise in the 40+ age group. Besides, when you are feeling low and undesirable, being in competition with others is really not helpful.

> Many people who join online dating sites have not recovered from their former breakup. They keep dating and entering relationships which lead nowhere. The last thing you need is to become involved in a relationship which will not last and not bring you what you deserve.
>
> You have been rejected and you are still raw. Wait until you are able to face potential rejection without taking it personally.

- Take time to grieve, to mend your heart, to reflect
- Stay in the harbour and mend your sails
- Heal your heart
- Take some space to think and simply be
- Rediscover who you are
- Learn to be happy on your own.

Only then are you ready to date again.

Do not settle for second-best.

Be patient and wait for what you deserve.

Don't rush into anything.

13
Steady yourself: hints and tips

When everything appears gloomy and negative around you, it is worth trying a few hints and tips designed to bring you solace and hope.

Start a journal

Every day, write down your thoughts – all of them – the good and the bad. It forms part of the process of releasing all your negative thoughts in complete confidence. By writing, you are releasing your fears. With time this will help you begin to gain some perspective and start moving to a more positive mindset.

When you read your journal again in the future, you will be surprised to see how far you have come.

Move!

Stretch your body. It will relieve the tension (watch those shoulders).

Get out for a walk: enjoy the fresh air and the exercise. Let the endorphins flow.

You also open yourself to the possibility of bumping into someone you know and having a chat. Good for your perspective too.

Breathe!

Practise deep breathing.

When we are stressed, we tend to take rapid shallow breaths into the top of our chest, which can make us feel panicky.

Act confident

Even if you do not feel it, ACT confident: shoulders back, head high, stand tall and smile. Like smiling into a mirror, pretending to be confident and adopting a confident bodily stance sends positive messages to the instinctive part of your brain, which then triggers the release of calming hormones.

When you feel panicky, sit with your feet firmly on the ground and your hands on your knees. Relax, breathe gently, feel that you are becoming more grounded, and visualise yourself being confident.

Talk to yourself in the mirror with your positive statements – I can do this, I am attractive, etc.

Visualise

Remember a time when you were happy, confident and in control. Remember how that felt.

Take the time to connect with the feeling.

Hold on to that picture in your mind and enjoy the feeling.

Find an 'anchor': an object you can touch, an image you can recall to connect again with this feeling, which in turn reminds you of better times. This exercise is helpful when you start having negative thoughts about yourself. By using an anchor, you can change your state of mind and regain calm when provoked.

Anchors can be: an item of jewellery that you can touch easily (a ring, a necklace), a crystal, a key fob. Any object that you like and that you can carry easily (it should not have any association with your former partner). When you touch your anchor, the emotional centre in your brain remembers the happy state and will help you deal with difficult times.

Become more self-aware

If you could, what would you say to your former partner?

Say it out loud or write it down in a letter. This is cathartic. Go for it and spare nothing, but DO NOT send it. This is only a means of letting off steam and putting the past behind.

Develop gratitude: this builds resilience

Think daily of the positive aspects of your life. What are they? What always makes you feel good?

Recall the positive moments of your day: a sunset, a smile from a toddler, a phone call from a friend, and the first daffodils in the park…

Write them in a 'gratitude diary' if you like. Say thank you. Express your gratitude.

Happiness

> If you don't like something, change it. If you can't change it, change your attitude. *Maya Angelou*

Remember that you are the source of your own happiness. To some extent we have some control over our happiness. No one else is responsible for this. No one can 'make you happy' or unhappy; it is up to you.

You may not have control of the situation you find yourself in, but you certainly have control over how you feel and react to it. Your thoughts, feelings and behaviours are all interlinked. By changing your behaviour (doing something physically different) you can change the way you feel and you can change the way you think. In the same way, if you change the way you think, you automatically change the way you behave and feel etc.

A lot of research has been done on happiness. Happiness has little to do with material success, making money, owning things.

We can increase our happiness levels because we have control of its essential elements. Most of these are linked to how we relate to other people and how we position ourselves:

- Be altruistic and do good things for others. Random acts of kindness have a huge positive impact on our wellbeing, as do speaking kindly of people and being genuinely interested in others
- Keep focused on the present, do not dwell on what has happened in the past, and stop worrying unnecessarily about the future. Stay in the present
- Clarify your values (what truly matters to you) and your strengths (what you are good at)
- Forgiveness has physical and emotional benefits for the person who forgives. Forgiving lowers tension, anger and stress and therefore has tangible physical benefits
- Generosity has an effect on our social connections, so being altruistic is really important
- Gratitude (counting our blessings)
- Positivity makes us happier; it releases dopamine in our brain. Being positive is definitely linked to happiness. Happy people look at adversity in a different way: they do not take setbacks personally; instead they see them as opportunities to grow
- To top it all, happiness is contagious!

Happiness is not a station you arrive at, but a manner of travelling.
Margaret Rumbeck

Laugh!

Laughter is truly the best medicine! It fools your mind into thinking that you are happy. Keep in touch with the friends who make you feel good and those who make you laugh. Think about young children who laugh so easily. Find reasons to laugh every day.

Reframing

- Start thinking about who you were when you first met your partner. What were you like then?

- What other difficult situations have you come through in your life?
- How did you overcome the problems then?
- Can you use the same skills and techniques now?

You have overcome many problems in your life, and you can overcome this.

Moving on to better things

- What did you previously enjoy doing that you have not done for ages?
- What has always been on your personal 'to-do' list that you have never got round to doing?
- Write it down
- How can you make it happen?

14
Affirmations

Affirmations are sentences to repeat to yourself (or say out loud) when you are feeling fragile.

They are designed to:

- Alleviate feelings of panic, loneliness and despair
- Bring back a feeling of calm
- Remind you that bad times will pass and better times will come.

Use these any time you are feeling upset and feel you need support. Find among the suggestions below the positive affirmations which will help you best.

Say to yourself three times –

- I can survive this
- It will pass
- I am staying in the 'not-knowing'
- I can and I will
- I accept myself as I am and I can deal with this
- Every day I am finding new ways to cope
- Every day I learn how to accept what I cannot change or control
- Every day I take steps to regain control of my life.

You can make up your own affirmations. If you do, always be sure to use positive language – never use negative words. For instance, don't say 'I'm going to stop feeling sorry for myself' – say: 'I'm going to feel happier/more confident today'.

The word 'today' is important. It gives you a timeframe. It cuts the 'impossible' task into bite-sized and therefore manageable chunks. Once you feel you have achieved that bit, then you move to the next one and so on.

Any difficult change is achieved one little step at a time.

Conclusion:

WHAT HAVE YOU LEARNT?

Remember that sometimes, not getting what you want is a wonderful stroke of luck. Dalai Lama XIV

One morning, you wake up and you realise that you are starting to feel better.

You are emerging from the chaos, and in effect you have started rebuilding your life. A year down the line, you will be surprised to realise how far you have travelled. You may still feel regret and sadness, but not the desperation of the early days. You are moving forward.

Well done! A new life is beginning, the life you choose. You now have the opportunity to start a better life!

Time to pause and think: what have you learnt?

Take stock: it is important not to make the same mistakes in the future. What was your role in the breakup? Were you too obsessed by your children, did you lose your sense of self? Did you take too much for granted?

Take time out, just to be.

Do not jump into another relationship for the sake of not being alone.

Instead: rediscover who you really are, what your values are. Be clear about what matters, what is acceptable to you (or not) in a future relationship. Do not settle for less than what you deserve.

It is important that you take time to reflect on what *you* have actually learnt from this experience and congratulate yourself on coming out the other end – you did it and you deserve a pat on the back – celebrate that success!